The publisher of this book is generously donating all royalties from the retail sales of **"STRESS-FREE DIVORCE VOLUME 01"** to:

JUNIOR ACHIEVEMENT

Junior Achievement is the nation's largest organization dedicated to giving young people the knowledge and skills they need to own their economic success, plan for their futures, and make smart academic and economic choices.

Junior Achievement was founded in 1919 by Theodore Vail, president of American Telephone & Telegraph; Horace Moses, president of Strathmore Paper Co.; and Senator Murray Crane of Massachusetts. Its first program, *JA Company Program®*, was offered to high school students on an after-school basis.

In 1975, the organization entered the classroom with the introduction of Project Business for the middle grades. Over the last 39 years, Junior Achievement has expanded its activities and broadened its scope to include in-school and after-school students.

Junior Achievement reaches more than 4.8 million students per year in 209,651 classrooms and after-school locations. JA programs are taught by volunteers in inner cities, suburbs, and rural areas throughout the United States, by 109 Area Offices in all 50 states.

You can learn more about
Junior Achievement by visiting
http://JuniorAchievement.org

STRESS-FREE DIVORCE
VOLUME 01

Leading Divorce Professionals Speak

VOLUME ONE

By Remarkable Press™

Stress-Free Divorce Volume 01/ Mark Imperial. —1st ed.

Managing Editor/ Stewart Andrew Alexander

ISBN: 978-0-9987085-1-5

CONTENTS

A NOTE TO THE READER

Thank you for buying your copy of "Stress-Free Divorce Volume 01: Leading Divorce Professionals Speak". This book was originally created as a series of live interviews, that's why it reads like a series of conversations, rather than a traditional book that talks *at you.*

I wanted you to feel as though the participants and I are talking *with you*, much like a close friend, or relative, and felt that creating the material this way would make it easier for you to grasp the topics and put them to use quickly, rather than wading through hundreds of pages.

So relax, grab a pen and paper, take notes and get ready to learn some fascinating, stress-free divorce insights.

Warmest regards,

Mark Imperial
Author and Radio Personality

INTRODUCTION

"Stress-Free Divorce volume 01: Leading Divorce Professionals Speak is a collaborative book series featuring leading Divorce Professionals from across the country.

Remarkable Press™ would like to extend a heartfelt thank you to all participants who took the time to submit their chapter and offer their support in becoming 'get the word out ambassadors' for this project.

100% of the royalties from the retail sales of this book will be donated to Junior Achievement. Should you want to make a direct donation, visit their website at: http://JuniorAchievement.org

ADAM WAITKEVICH

A Conversation with Adam Waitkevich
CFP®, AIF®, CDFA™, ADFA® - President and
Founder, Divorce Financial Solutions (DFS)

Divorce Financial Solutions, LLC are experts in divorce finances. They help divorcing couples avoid costly financial mistakes so they spend less money during the process, and enter their post-divorce lives with more confidence and on greater financial footing.

Tell us about Divorce Financial Solutions (DFS) and the types of clients you serve?

Adam Waitkevich: We help individuals, couples and divorce professionals by bringing specialized financial expertise into the divorce process. Our work lends an empowering clarity and focus to the process of dividing marital income, assets and debt, which leads to a more efficient divorce process with more positive financial outcomes.

Divorce is an emotional and often overwhelming life event and many couples struggle to organize finances and make sound choices about their future within that fast-paced setting. Typically, divorcing individuals find difficulty in making a commitment to a final agreement because their biggest questions remain unanswered. "is this a fair agreement?"; "am I getting a good/bad deal? "; "Have I looked at all the options?"; "is this a settlement that will work for me today AND in the future?" Our process and expertise provides answers to those very questions, which helps to eliminate uncertainty and allow couples to arrive at better decisions sooner. With each divorce, we help to identify and organize the many complexities and deliver them in a simplified and workable manner where parties can make well-informed decisions. Similarly, we help legal professionals reduce their liability and become stronger advocates for their clients by providing optimal financial solutions.

What are the biggest misconceptions about the role your service provides in a stress-free Divorce?

Adam Waitkevich: The biggest misconception would be that our services may not be applicable to their particular divorce. There is a notion that only high-net-worth couples require a financial expert to assist with the divorce process. I believe that every divorce can benefit from financial expertise regardless of the level of assets involved. Divorce should be viewed as an extension of financial planning. At its core, the divorce process is the dismantling of all prior planning, building, saving, growing that was done for a SINGLE household that now needs to be dismantled and reassembled so that it works for TWO new and separate households. While a high-net-worth couple may certainly have more complex issues to address, every individual or couple can benefit from financial guidance with their divorce. Unintended mistakes are made every day in divorce regardless of net worth. Mistakes in a lower-income/net-worth divorce may be more financially harmful as there is less room for error.

What are some little known pitfalls or common mistakes you see being made with divorce couples you have worked with?

Adam Waitkevich: Unrealistic expectations. This is one of the most common pitfalls, but the easiest to overcome. I see two primary examples of misconceptions and expectations.

Unrealistic Financial Expectations - I work with many divorcing individuals that enter the process with unrealistic expectations about how they believe final outcome will turn out. More specifically, many individuals arrive to the negotiation process with false or inaccurate information as to how a particular income (child support/alimony) or asset (pension plan, stock options, and social security) will be divided. This is quite normal and not unexpected given that most of us do not have professional experience with divorce, but also do to the fact that too much merit is given to advice from friends and family regarding their prior experience or "expertise". The good news is that divorce financial expertise can quickly address any misinformation and put the process back on track. The primary downside to this dilemma is the added stress and disappointment experienced while adjusting expectations downward that were too optimistic. While ultimately, this is not financially harmful, it can be very upsetting and difficult to process, which can add additional burden to the emotional strain already inherent with divorce.

My advice in avoiding this dilemma is to seek professional advice early on, try not to not place too great an emphasis on hearsay or the divorce experience of friends and family, and take time to get education on your local divorce laws and more realistic outcomes. If it sounds too good (or bad) to be true, it just may be. Keep an open mind but tempered expectations until things settle out. Your divorce can be better if you enter with firm but realistic expectations.

Professional Expectations - I have also witnessed a general notion or expectation that one can arrive at an optimal divorce settlement relying only on a single divorce professional – family law attorney, divorce mediator, or financial expert. In my years as a divorce financial expert, I have had the benefit of working with dozens of amazingly bright and competent family law attorneys and divorce mediators. With that said, none of those divorce professionals would be on my list of names to call for financial advice. While I know I am not alone in that thought, we all know someone who has done exactly that – left all their important choices (financial and otherwise) to be decided largely by family law attorneys and the courts. More surprisingly, people continue to take that path today and expect optimal results (and we still wonder why so many divorcees feel like they got a bad deal).

To be fair in this analogy, as a financial expert, I always utilize the expertise of open-minded and professional divorce attorneys with each of my clients as they provide a necessary skillset that I do not have. The takeaway here is to remember what expertise each professional is qualified to bring to the divorce. Successful divorces today often involve numerous specialist, each bringing unique but focused expertise, which allows for more beneficial outcomes and a more efficient process. Today, more than ever, divorcing couples need to recognize that positive long-term benefits will come from using a collaborative approach in divorce.

Shortsightedness - Forgetting to plan for the future. This is a very common and often unintentional mistake that stems from a hyper-focus on the division of current assets and debt without consideration of the transition period (next 1-3 years post-divorce) and beyond (retirement years). In many cases, once the marital property has been identified and laid out, the parties take the next logical step, which is entering into back-and-forth negotiations over their "stake". While this is a necessary part of any divorce, it is often approached blindly without consideration of post-divorce lifestyle or budget.

This approach will very likely lead to less optimal outcomes in the future and in the worst cases lead to financial devastation. In most divorces, somebody will be moving out and funds will be needed for a new home, first/last rent and possibly new furnishings. Additionally, there may be debt to be paid off related to the marriage or even the divorce process itself. Very few individuals I have worked with have taken the time to prepare a realistic post-divorce budget. In most cases, expenses and lifestyle will have significant changes.

How can one decide on what asset(s) are best for them in the divorce settlement if they have not considered their long-term outlook and needs? Even if the property division is equitable in dollar-terms, one party may learn they could have fared better by asking for more of the marital cash assets as compared to personal property or retirement assets, which are more expensive to liquidate. Unfortunately, in many cases this mistake or oversight will not be realized for several years after the divorce. While it is certainly not a normal thought process to contemplate and plan for retirement during the divorce process, it is crucial that some consideration is allotted to the next several years and even longer including retirement. It is always prudent to think about divorce as an opportunity to start fresh with your own financial planning. Decisions made in divorce are permanent and can shape your future for better or worse.

Ignoring or Misunderstanding Pension Plans - Unlike 401(k) Plans and IRA accounts, pension plans are not current assets that have nice, easy-to-read statements that indicate their value. Similar to social security benefits, pension plans are actually future streams of income to be received at retirement, which makes for a very daunting and abstract concept when attempting to value and divide pursuant to divorce.

Very often, and because of challenges and misunderstandings of pension plans, the first objective of the parties is to find a way to remove the pension from the process entirely. "I'll keep X and you keep your pension and we'll call it even". The thought with many couples is to first eliminate dealing with the pension at all, which is a huge mistake as the pension plan is often the most valuable marital asset with the exception of the marital home. Here is an example:

Years ago, a couple came to me to review their agreement before final signatures were completed. The husband had a state pension worth $80,000 based on a statement he had received. In exchange for keeping this pension, the husband was giving his wife an additional $40,000 from their savings account, which represented her half of the pension. There was no disagreement from either at the time we met as the terms were equitable.

What neither of them knew was that the statement that listed the pension value at $80,000 represented ONLY the husband's contributions to the plan and not the full value, which included a second and much larger contribution by the State. When the pension was analyzed to reflect its present value, the couple learned it was worth over $1,200,000 in present-value terms. Identifying this unintended error resulted in a significant and profound change for the better for the wife. The husband, who was equally confused about the pension, was pleased as his intentions was for an equitable and fair agreement.

EMOTION - The costliest enemy in divorce. Spitefulness is very common obstacle that presents itself throughout the process. The downside is added stress, time and cost to the process. Sadly, I have yet to witness any upside from highly emotional divorces. A recent conversation with a former client (she divorced four years ago) provided valuable insight into the power of emotions. This woman is highly educated and very successful. In her day-to-day life she is recognized as a strong and level-headed leader and here is what she said to me, "Looking back, I see how foolish we were to fight so blindly and spend so much money over what really amounted to things of no significance.

Today, with college tuition upon us, I realized that we quite literally spent the equivalent of 3 years' tuition on legal fees and we ended up no better off in the agreement. Although it is easy to look back and see my mistake, in THAT moment, all my rational thought was gone and I had a single focus to hold my ground at any cost." What struck me most in our conversation was just how powerful emotions can be to overcome in the moment. While I would really like to provide a fix-all solution to this dilemma, I cannot.

The best I can do is advise to try and slow the process down mentally, take extra time to think things through and understand that emotional obstacles will be part of the process. Perhaps understanding and expecting this ahead of time can be of some help to make better choices.

How can these pitfalls be avoided?

Adam Waitkevich: While each pitfall is challenging on its own, all of those mentioned can be minimized or avoided by making a conscious effort to ignore impulsive and emotion-based choices and to get educated about your finances. There are many long-term benefits to be reaped by taking the time to explore options during divorce.

Below is a short list of good habits:

- Don't be lazy. Do your own homework and seek help from experts where needed.

- Avoid emotion-based decisions whenever possible. Emotions will be part of the process, don't let them drive decision-making.

- Take time to prepare a post-divorce budget. Knowing what you need will help you make better and more confident decisions.

- Consider your long-term future when negotiating the settlement agreement.

- Treat divorce as a financial planning platform for your new life.

Will you describe a situation in which you've helped a couple overcome a misconception or unknown pitfall in working toward a stress-free divorce?

Adam Waitkevich: Several years ago I worked with a couple that had been separated for over 4 years without an agreement or concrete terms to move forward. During that 4-year period, the couple worked with several divorce mediators and dozens of mediation sessions and churned through several family law attorneys as well.

When I met them, they both (understandably) had reservations as to how effective a divorce financial expert would be in getting them closer to a final agreement they could both live with. After our first session of 2-hours, the dynamics changed entirely. Because we focused exclusively on the financial aspect and utilized simple yet accurate illustrations, the couple was able to get re-engaged and motivated to push through their prior sticking points. Our success was not necessarily due to poor legal advice received over the years, but rather the couple's inability to find a method that pushed through the emotional roadblock they created. Once the ambiguity of future dollars and alimony payments and budgets were brought into focus, they were able to quickly finalize an agreement that worked for both of them.

While the remainder of our work together still involved emotions and numerous adjustments, the ability to stay focused on concrete financials was enough to prevent the onset of emotion-based debating over property division. In this case, numbers and facts helped shift their focus away from the endless circle of emotion-based road to nowhere.

What inspired you to become a Divorce Financial Expert?

Adam Waitkevich: At the risk of sounding cliché, I derive a high level of personal satisfaction from helping others with financial matters. Given the success I experienced with clients of our financial planning firm Coppertree® , the transition to divorce finances made perfect sense. I did, however, experience a divorce situation with one of our financial planning clients back in 2009 that was instrumental in my ultimate pursuit of divorce-related credentials and skills.

This client had just retired and we had recently completed his income and investment planning for the next several years when divorce entered the picture. Over the next two years, I watched as my client slowly succumbed to the draining process of his divorce, writing check after check to pay for legal fees.

Each time I asked for updates and why he continued paying so much, he responded dispiritedly that he was "done fighting" and just paying (praying) to be done. Further discussions with this client confirmed that there was no planning or process being used to improve his divorce process. It was then that I began my research into the divorce arena in hopes to improve the process for others.

Can you share a lesson you learned early on, that still impacts how you perform your service today?

Adam Waitkevich: Early on, I recognized that there is much more emotion surrounding divorce finances as compared to traditional financial planning. I learned immediately that Divorce is highly disruptive to the individuals and families involved and I learned quickly to take a more empathetic role while still providing practical and accurate financial guidance. Because of the unique emotional dynamic in divorce, I obtained my divorce mediation training certification. The skills I learned through mediation training has helped me be a better "financial-mediator" and ultimately improve the process for my divorcing clients.

What is the one thing that we may not have covered that you could share with someone who is wanting a successful, stress-free divorce?

Adam Waitkevich: I think it is important to mention that my work as a divorce financial expert is complementary to all divorce methods and not intended to be a replacement for legal expertise. There is sometimes confusion as to where a divorce financial expert fits in the process and the answer is anywhere there are financial matters to work through. I have found it most beneficial if my work is incorporated early in the process as it will generally increase efficiency and reduce total time and money commitment. Additionally, while I pick on family law practitioners for their lack of financial acumen, most of my success can be attributed to the many great family law professionals who I collaborate with on a regular basis.

Can you address some common misconceptions, or reasons potential couples that could benefit from working with a divorce financial specialist like yourself might chose NOT to?

Adam Waitkevich: They believe their lawyer can handle the finances.

Family Law attorneys go to school to become experts in family law, not financial matters. A common misconception is that the courts and legal professionals can handle all divorce matters as this has been the norm for decades. Today, more and more individuals and family law professionals have recognized the tangible benefits to adding outside financial expertise to the divorce process. If you work with an attorney unwilling to use financial expertise, find a new attorney.

They think "We don't have millions of dollars and property to divide. We don't need a financial expert."

This is also a misconception. I have helped many lower-income families avoid thousands of dollars in unintended financial mistakes. Small items recognized during the process can save many thousands in future mistakes. The risk is much higher in NOT using a financial expert.

They believe their current financial planner can help them.

There is an important distinction to understand between a CFP (Certified Financial Planner) professional and a divorce financial professional. Despite the robust financial planning and investment knowledge a CFP practitioner holds, he/she does not have sufficient and expert training as it related to divorce and divorce finances. Specifically, divorcing individuals should seek a professional with the CDFA (Certified Divorce Financial Analyst) or ADFA (Advanced Divorce Financial Analyst) credentials. Both designations are sponsored by the Institute of Divorce Financial Analysts (www.institutedfa.com), which was founded in 1993. The IDFA is the premier national organization dedicated to the certification, education and promotion of the use of financial divorce professionals in the divorce arena. Hiring an expert with the CDFA or ADFA credentials can assure there is intimate knowledge of divorce finances. I believe the most ideal expert would be an individual holding their CFP designation as well as the divorce-credentials as there is often overlap with complex financial matters during divorce.

They think that adding another expert will be too expensive.

In most of my cases, there are quantifiable savings to be recognized that more than offsets the resources spent on the process. In some cases, the mistakes avoided were worth many times the total cost of the divorce. The better question to ask is, "What are the potential costs to not getting professional help?"

They think they can do it themselves because they work with finances.

I have had great success in cases where the husband or wife are financially savvy. There are two main benefits to hiring an outside expert in such cases.

1.) You overcome the trust factor. It is much easier for the party with lower financial acumen to trust a neutral party during the process as compared to the spouse they are divorcing.

2.) Objectivity – Similarly, a financial neutral can provide alternate suggestions and help to bring both parties on equal footing with respect to decision making knowledge and do so in an impartial way.

How can someone find out more and connect with you?

Adam Waitkevich: Please call me directly to talk at 508-839-3730. Making a personal connection is always the most efficient way to learn more and to determine if our service is right for you.

They can also find more information at my website: www.divorcefinancialsolutions.net.

KAREN D. SPARKS

A Conversation with
Karen D. Sparks, CDFA™, J.D
Divorce Financial Strategists™

If you or someone you know is contemplating or currently involved in the divorce process, understanding and implementing the appropriate financial analysis for marital assets and spousal/family support is vital.

Karen D. Sparks, CDFA™, J.D. is the principal and owner of Divorce Financial Strategists™ located in Santa Clara, CA. In this chapter, she will be providing her professional insight on approaching the area of spousal/alimony/maintenance support.

Ms. Sparks' practice goal is simple: Providing a neutral environment for those in divorce/separation to work through the allocation of their marital assets and develop a process to approach spousal/family support issues.

She serves clients locally throughout the state of California and nationwide for all aspects of divorce and separation financial analysis as well as post-divorce financial implications.

Ms. Sparks is a member of the San Mateo County Bar Association, the Institute of Divorce Financial Analysts™, and is both a member and director on the Board of Directors for the Association of Divorce Financial Planners. She also contributes to the Wevorce organization as a certified financial architect.

THE PATH TO SOLVING SOME OF THE CHALLENGES OF SPOUSAL SUPPORT

One of the biggest mental hurdles that individuals face in approaching spousal support is increased anxiety about their ability to maintain their current lifestyle and further, what will happen if this is not possible. I usually receive a good deal of questions from the perspective of the payor (the spouse providing support) and the payee (the spouse receiving support).

From the viewpoint of the payor, common questions include:

- How much support will I have to pay and how long will I have to pay it?

- Can I reduce my payment by requiring the other party to obtain employment?

- What happens if I can no longer maintain the agreed upon level of support due to loss of employment, reduced compensation, disability, illness or retirement?

From the viewpoint of the payee common questions include:

- How much support am I entitled to and will I have to pay taxes on this income?

- Can I accept the value of other marital assets in lieu of support?

- Can my support payments be used as income to obtain credit and/or qualify for a lease or mortgage obligation?

In addition to these questions, some individuals are confused and uncertain about the role that a certified divorce finance analyst can play in facilitating and providing effective solutions for the support discussion, which can become very emotional and challenging.

The way that I try to ease this state of mind for my clients is to outline my role as a partner with them by following these four key approaches:

1. Collaboration and education on the traditional and creative ways to approach spousal support and marital asset allocation in divorce;

2. Dedication to their goals and objectives during and after divorce;

3. Financial focus that intersects with and supports other divorce/separation team members such as attorneys, mediators, wealth managers etc. and

4. Adherence to a standard of client meeting conversations that is respectful and productive.

The key is to ensure that my clients are educated and confirmed in the decisions involving support and the marital assets.

I try to communicate my firm believe in the following mental journey: *Knowledge reduces stress. The absence of stress leads to more informed decisions. The ability to make informed decisions results in an atmosphere of confidence and peace of mind. Peace of mind allows you to live life strong during and after divorce.*

Now, let's take a look at some client case studies to illustrate how some of the more common spousal support issues can be addressed. (Note: names and personal data have been changed for privacy and security)

Case Study #1- Alice and David

Alice and David have been married for 26 years. There were two children of this union. At the time these clients consulted me, they had just initiated their divorce proceedings. At issue here was the fact that during a majority of the marriage, David was the high wage earner and Alice was a registered nurse.

Key issues concerned the fact that David preferred to negotiate a monthly support payment for the statutory period required by law as he wanted to take advantage of the tax deduction aspect against his salary.

Alice did not want the risk that something could happen to David and/or his employment and wanted a solution that made her feel more comfortable.

The couple had acquired additional real estate outside the United States a few years prior to the divorce with a plan to further develop this into other opportunities. Since they were no longer going to do this as a couple, we looked to some alternatives.

After I conducted considerable analysis of their assets and presented options for the allocation and any possible tax implications thereof, they agreed on an amount for a buyout of the support obligation.

This option provided Alice with more security and flexibility and David weighed his options and decided that not having to continue to consider monthly payments into the future was better for his lifestyle.

Case Study #2- Tom

Tom came to me for post-divorce analysis. There are four children of the marriage, all of whom are 18 or over. Tom and his wife had previously negotiated a marital settlement agreement with their mediator and spousal support was based on their respective salaries at the time the divorce became final a few years ago. The agreement for Tom to pay spousal support ends in approximately 8 years.

However, recently Tom's ex-wife elected to leave her employment of long standing and to date has not found another position to replace it.

The couple informally agreed on an adjusted support amount for this interim period, but Tom wanted to present his ex-wife with a more reliable scenario that takes into account their current situation.

I worked with Tom to produce an analytical formula that we validated for various outcomes which would be reliable for both parties and that would take the guesswork out of how to proceed going forward.

Case Study #3- Debra and Colton

Debra and Colton had been married for almost 26 years with two college age children. Debra achieved a degree in the technology field and Colton had achieved undergraduate and graduate level education in the biology field.

Colton continued in his career after their marriage and it was agreed that Debra would become the President of Domestic Operations (aka- the stay at home parent).

I was retained to prepare analysis for Debra by an attorney whom I had worked with on a previous case with another client. The matter of spousal support was set for a court trial. Colton's attorney also retained their own expert.

There were many challenging issues in this case which included but were not limited to, how soon Debra could enter the job market, the value of other marital assets affecting the term and amount of spousal support, the amount of current necessary expenses incurred by Debra and what efforts Debra was making to become marketable for employment as soon as possible, etc.

In this case it was necessary for me to perform a marital standard of living analysis also known as a lifestyle analysis. This is a process by which I engage in a comprehensive financial review and analysis of the marriage over a set period of time.

The goal is to produce a number that results in a baseline figure for support that represents an appropriate amount of monthly support for the receiving spouse.

With the value of the other marital assets including Colton's substantial retirement accounts, I was able to establish and validate their standard of living such that the monthly amount for Debra would provide a comfortable income for support for the statutory period provided by law as re-employment at a significant salary level was going to be challenging for her to achieve at the time of my analysis.

It is important to note that all client circumstances have their own unique blueprint. These case studies illustrate a few of the custom approaches that I have found useful to apply in sorting out the best and most agreeable path to resolve the issue of spousal support for families.

SUMMARY

I choose to do this work professionally because in addition to working with families towards a reasonable outcome, I journeyed through my own very difficult divorce. More than anything, I want to empower individuals to be smart about the divorce financial process and additionally, I want to make sure that we go over and outline their requirements and goals post-divorce.

Divorce finances can actually be complicated on some levels and require the specific application of certain analytical processes. Try to avoid the DIY method of determining computations for value, division etc. among yourselves as these are often not based on appropriate guidelines and can lead to adverse decisions and consequences.

CONCLUSION

You can contact Karen D. Sparks, CDFA™, J.D. at Divorce Financial Strategists™ by phone at 650-201-6311 or email, cdfa@divorcefinancialstrategists.com. Mention the "Stress-Free Divorce" and receive a 20% discount on your initial consultation fee- this is a $60.00 value!

JOHN P. CITO

A Conversation with John P. Cito
Certified Divorce Financial Analyst™ (CDFA)

Divorce has many components, one of which is the financial side. When financial issues are combined with emotions, the results can be devastating. Asset and debt distribution affects every aspect of your life. Plan for your divorce the way you planned for your wedding.

What looks equal today in a settlement may not be fair five or ten years from now once factors such as inflation, increases in the cost of living, taxes etc. are considered. Will your divorce leave you broke?

CDFA, John Cito, Certified Divorce Financial Analyst™ focuses on the components of pre- and post-divorce financial planning. Divorce Planning is a specialized form of financial planning that can help you achieve a financially fair divorce settlement by analyzing the proposals of you and your spouse.

CDFA is not legal advice. Using mathematics and certain assumptions, your assets that are to be divided as well as your lifestyle will be analyzed and evaluated. The goal is to help make your divorce process humane, civilized, and compassionate.

Tell us about your divorce financial planning practice and the divorcing women you serve.

John Cito: Marriage is about love and divorce is about money. I help divorcing women by simplifying the complexity of their financial situation. Then I help them develop a strategy to obtain the best settlement and serve as their personal Chief Financial Officer to handle their financial issues after divorce.

What do you feel are the biggest myths or misconceptions about how a CDFA plays in a stress free divorce? Or Challenges that I hear my clients face?

John Cito: First and foremost, many people have never heard of a Certified Divorce Financial Analyst. I have heard on numerous occasions "I wish I had you when I was getting divorced". In addition, I invariably get asked questions such as "SO you are a mediator?" NO! Or Are you a forensic accountant, once again NO!

There are numerous challenges that my clients face. When your marriage is over and a divorce is inevitable, the common knee jerk reaction is to call a lawyer. Since every divorce is different, now is the time that they have to assess their situation. It can be amicable and turn hostile and vice versa.

When it is time to seek a lawyer, choosing the wrong one can be costly, in more ways than one. Now is time to do your homework.

I had a case where my client hired a personal injury attorney to handle her divorce – not advisable. Another challenge is not listening to other people about their divorce. They aren't going to tell you 100% of the details. A divorce is unique and time will be better spent focusing on the details of your own divorce.

What are some of the most common fears people have about having a stress free divorce working with a CDFA?

John Cito: There are no fears, just some confusion as to the role I play. Their lawyer knows the law, their accountant know taxes. To me, it's all about educating the client and explaining the financial aspect of their divorce and the impact that outcome will have on their lives going forward.

Examples are budget preparation and lifestyle analysis. I always tell my clients that they have to plan their divorce with the same concentration on the details that they did when they planned their wedding.

What are some of the common mistakes that are made when trying to have a stress free divorce that you would like to make people aware of.

John Cito: Let me share a few examples.

1. Choosing the wrong attorney

2. Listening to friends and relatives about their divorce

3. Having unrealistic expectations

4. Spending money arguing over something that has no meaning and being spiteful.

5. Trying to hide money. Majority of it can be found and waste money on experts' fees.

6. Implement a pre-divorce check list.

How have you been able to help divorcing women overcome these obstacles?

John Cito: The initial meeting is designed where the divorcing spouse and I interview each other and it enables me to get a clear picture of the situation along with the issues and concerns. We go over the length of the marriage, which party initiated the divorce, family dynamics and determine the ideal desired result.

Mrs. A decided to file for divorce after 11 years of marriage. Mr. A, 10 years her senior handled all of the household finances, paying the bills and establishing a budget. He also managed their retirement accounts and investments. Mrs. A who has always worked needed help understanding the financial statements and a financial break down of assets.

During our Mastering Your Divorce Agenda, we performed an asset evaluation and categorized them from retirement to non-retirement along with pre and post marital status. The results are then written up in an easy to understand comprehensive report.

After the lawyers drew up the settlement agreement, prior to it being signed, a settlement audit was performed. The audit reviews the alimony, child support and equitable distribution components of the settlement.

What inspired you to become a Certified Divorce Financial Analyst?

John Cito: I established my own company after working for the Wall Street firms and in 2003 I had four women referred to me who were recently divorced. The referrals came from four different sources and no one knew of the other. Combine that with my parent's divorce while I was in college. This was at a time there wasn't any financial help available that focused on divorce financial issues.

At this time I decided to focus on specialize in divorce financial planning instead of a general financial planning practice.

The ability to help a divorcing woman from the beginning to the end of her divorce and thereafter is very rewarding. Especially educating her on the financial issues and how everything will affect her future.

Can you share a lesson you learned early on, that still impacts how you perform your service today?

John Cito: I witnessed financial professionals entering divorce financial planning and yet maintain a general practice. This is an area that you must specialize in. Granted, the post-divorce financial planning incorporates all of components of a financial plan. However, to get to that point, one has to specialize in the foundation and fundamentals of the financial issues of divorce.

Also, I learned to put a strong professional team together. I have a team of CPAs, Forensic Accountants, Business Valuators, Insurance Experts and Mental Health Professionals.

What is the one thing that we may not have covered that you could share with someone who is wanting a successful stress free divorce?

John Cito: Be proactive and master your divorce. Remember, your lawyer works for you, I work for you, other professionals that may be involved in your divorce work for you. If you have questions, ASK, if you aren't happy with certain events, SPEAK UP. Make sure that you understand and are comfortable with the results that you are getting.

By working with me as a CDFA, you will empower and educate and yourself on the financial components that will affect your financial situation today and the years to come. Divorce has many components, one of which is the financial side. When financial issues are combined with emotions, the results can be devastating. I will show you how to take control of your divorce.

How can someone find out more and connect with you?

John Cito: Go to my web site www.divorceplan.com and download the free report and listen to the podcast. I have offices in Bergen and Monmouth County New Jersey and Bethlehem, Pa. or call 888-379-9569

The cost of the initial consultation is to bring me supplies that I can send to our Troops in Afghanistan. A $30.00 visit to the dollar store for q tips, razors, tooth brushes and tooth paste, baby wipes, beef jerky, hand warmers, feminine products are the most requested items. I pay for the postage and ship the items to the Troops.

JORYN JENKINS

A Conversation with Joryn Jenkins
Open Palm Law

Who is Joryn Jenkins?

Joryn Jenkins: I'm an attorney who's been trying cases for 35 years. Over the years, I've seen how divorce court can ruin people, not just financially, but also emotionally. When I learned about collaborative law, I just knew that this was the right thing, and I wanted to be a part of it.

The sign in front of my building used to say "Joryn Jenkins & Associates, Trial Attorneys." Now it says "Open Palm Law."

So what exactly is Collaborative Law?

Joryn Jenkins: It's a process for resolving disputes without going to court. Each party retains his own lawyer. The lawyers get together and hire a facilitator (or coach) and a financial person, both also collaboratively-trained.

Everyone on the team agrees to the ground rules, which include that they will settle the issues privately, without resort to court.

The average divorce will bankrupt most people and causes hatred that lasts forever. The Open Palm Divorce is private, cheaper, quicker, safer, less stressful, and less likely to cause hard feelings. We call it the kinder, gentler divorce. Simply put, the husband and wife, and their lawyers, work together without going to court. They hire "middlemen," who help the process. If it all works out, then the divorce is done quickly and easily, and saves everyone money and grief.

How does it work?

Joryn Jenkins: Collaborative divorce takes place over a series of meetings, as many as are necessary:

- Between each client and each neutral professional;

- Between each client and his or her lawyer; and

- Of the full team of clients and professionals.

No judge; no court. This is the heart of the Open Palm Divorce: if the parties throw in the towel and file in court, their lawyers are off the case. The clients must retain new lawyers to go to court.

Thus, the collaborative lawyers are completely focused on helping the parties reach agreement; they are not distracted by the need to gird themselves for battle. No lawyers "stirring the pot" or "churning the case."

Why are you so excited about Collaborative Law?

Joryn Jenkins: Because it's a positive change, a change for the better! Today, when someone files for divorce, it's always a race to the courthouse, because the first to file has the advantage. And it's war from the get-go; that petition for divorce is always a shot across the bow. It's destructive, not only financially, but also emotionally.

And, if there are children, they are always caught in the middle. Even when my client "wins," it never feels like we won.

Unlike traditional divorce, the Open Palm Divorce is constructive. First, neither party has the advantage; they are always on equal footing. And, instead of being adversaries, the lawyers serve as teachers and problem-solvers in a quest to create the best possible resolution for both parties. The parties learn to problem solve, to identify what they need instead of just talking about what they want.

What do you mean? How does that work?

Joryn Jenkins: We work to identify the parties' underlying concerns, rather than what they say they want, so...

"I want the house" really means "I want security," "I want the best schools for my kids," "I want to be close to my neighbors"

"I want the kids 90% of the time" means "I don't want to pay you child support"

And "I want 50% of everything," means "I want my fair share."

How does this differ from mediation?

Joryn Jenkins: Mediation is an event; the purpose of mediation is to get the parties to compromise enough to end their marriage. And mediation is a free look at the other side's case, in case you end up in trial. Mediation is confidential, but, if you go to trial anyway, you can still use the information you discovered during mediation.

Collaborative law is a process; the parties learn how to problem solve and how to move forward. If they have children, they learn to work together in their continuing and different relationship as co-parents.

Why?

Joryn Jenkins: Because it's not over, even when it's over; for example, you are always parents together, like it or not. You choose Open Palm, in part, because it's not just about the divorce!

Why are you so gung-ho about this?

Joryn Jenkins: "50% of first marriages... 67% of second marriages... and 73% of third marriages end in divorce." Divorce is rampant today. Like a stone thrown into a pond, court divorce has an adverse impact on everyone, because it ripples outward. Not only on the parties, but on their children, the grandparents, their neighbors, their employers... Everyone!

I made this point to a banker I met recently, and he replied that his neighbor had subpoenaed him to testify just the week before!

And no one learns anything in the process. Not only do people get divorced again and again, but, even after their divorce is over, they go back to court again and again!

On the other hand, the Open Palm Divorce will teach folks how to problem solve, how to work with each other to resolve their disputes. And it will equip them with techniques to work through problems they may have in their future relationships. It even sometimes helps them to solve the problems in their current relationship; I've heard of parties reconciling during the process!

Collaborative law is at the tipping point. And the ripple effect that collaborative law will have on our society can only be positive.

What are the pluses to Collaborative Law, aside from teaching people how to problem-solve?

Joryn Jenkins:

1. *It's confidential*

The parties' financial information;

The parties' family issues (dirty laundry like addictions, domestic violence, affairs, and mental health issues);

Look at the celebrities who have used collaborative divorce (Robin Williams, T'Boone Pickens, Madonna, Tiger Woods, Guy Ritchie, and Cameron Crowe).

Is it the same as "sealing" the court file?

Joryn Jenkins: No, generally, "sealing" just means that everything is placed in a manila envelope marked "sealed." Any with access to the file can still open the envelope. In collaborative law, the documents are never placed in the court file in the first place.

2. It's less expensive

How much does a court divorce cost?

Joryn Jenkins: Let me put it this way: it can cost as much as you want, but it can't cost as little as you want; it's not just in one party's control! I have seen everyday divorces that cost as much as $50-100,000 per spouse. I have seen people with millions of dollars spend over a million dollars each on their attorneys and expert witnesses.

What does the cost depend on?

Joryn Jenkins: A number of factors:

- Children

- House

- Alimony

- Business valuation

- Investments

- Retirement accounts

- Number of experts

- Age of the children

- Wealth and resources of the parties

- Pets (yes, I once represented a husband in a divorce where the only question was who would get the dogs...)

- But most importantly, the animosity between the parties!

What about the Open Palm Divorce?

Joryn Jenkins: Well, you know intuitively that it'll be less, just by its very nature.

Why?

Joryn Jenkins: None of that Perry Mason stuff! No discovery; no motions; no trial; no battle of the experts....

[Plus every team member does what he does best

The financial neutral works on the finances;

The facilitator works on the emotional issues;

The lawyers coach their clients on the legal issues and the problem solving]

3. *It's less stressful.*

Any divorce is difficult. The Open Palm Divorce is just easier. We call it the kinder, gentler divorce. People think of divorce as a legal process with an emotional component. In truth, it's an emotional process with a legal component. We ignore this truth in the court divorce; in the collaborative divorce, we recognize it by relying on the "coach" or "facilitator."

Who is the coach?

Joryn Jenkins: A mental health professional, who defuses the emotional bombs that explode during the court process.

4. *The Collaborative Process belongs to the parties*; not to the lawyers or to the judge. So scheduling is easier. The results can be personally tailored. The parties can do what judges cannot legally do. For example, in Florida, the parties can agree to pay for their kids' college; a judge could not order that.

In court, the judge is the center of attention and everyone addresses the judge. The parties and the lawyers never address each other.

In collaborative law, the parties are the center of attention and learn to communicate with each other. Instead of being adversarial and argumentative, the lawyers model good communication skills for their clients

What do the judges think of collaborative divorce?

Joryn Jenkins: Well, they love it, of course. They are supportive not only because they have more than enough work to do as it is, but because they know that their rulings are based on limited information.

How can you reduce a 15-year marriage with three children to a one-, maybe a two-day trial? People should make decisions based on their intimate knowledge of their families, rather than relying on a third party who, as a judge once explained to me, only sees a snapshot of their lives before deciding issues they will have to live with for the rest of their lives.

Is Collaborative Law limited to divorces?

Joryn Jenkins: Absolutely not. It is applicable to any dispute. It would obviously work in a partnership or corporate dispute, which is, after all, a business divorce. But we've also trained probate lawyers and employment attorneys in collaborative dispute resolution, as well. I can see the collaborative law process operating in any area where the parties disagree.

I understand that the collaborative process is a constructive approach to dissolution of marriage? Why do you say that?

Courtroom divorce is very destructive. Everyone knows that. It's war from the get-go. Collaborative divorce, on the other hand, is constructive, teaching the clients skills such as....

You say that your clients learn problem solving, communication, and partnering skills. How do you do that?

Joryn Jenkins: Part of the collaborative process involves individual client meetings with the facilitator. The facilitator is expert in these skills. The facilitator discusses these skills directly with the clients and sometimes even gives them homework to help them hone those skills. But the process also involves team meetings. At these meetings, the lawyers model these skills for their clients. The clients learn from the modeling that goes on in front of them, working through with the team, but also with each other, the very issues raised in their dissolution of marriage.

Joryn, what was your most touching experience in a collaborative divorce?

Joryn Jenkins: I've seen innumerable touching moments, if you will, and the one that probably gets me the most often, and which happens with surprising frequency, is when one of the spouses apologizes to the other. The time that really stands out in my mind was when I had the husband, he came to me and he said to me, "We don't have any children.

This just shouldn't be that tough, and I want to do it collaboratively because I want to be able to look in the mirror at myself when the divorce is done, and I know that litigation is just so awful. I also know that my wife doesn't want a divorce. I've moved out. I've been out of the house for six or eight months now and I can't seem to get her to go to a lawyer."

So I told him, "Fine. I'll send her my invitation, if you will, to join us in the collaborative environment to get the divorce done, and I'll send her the names of three lawyers I've worked with in the past and also the practice group website so that she can pick any lawyer she wants who's been trained collaboratively and we can go from there." I sent the letter and I didn't hear back, which is not unusual. I called her a couple of times, didn't get hold of her.

Of course, it's unusual for a lawyer to call an opposing party, but in collaborative divorce, they aren't really the opposing party, if you will. We don't think of them that way, and I wasn't going to talk about law to her, and she didn't have a lawyer so it was perfectly ethical, but I couldn't get hold of her anyway. So I sent her another letter, and she still ignored me. This went on for some time, and I counseled patience.

Then one day after several months, I mean it was four or six months. It was a long time. I get a phone call from the first guy on the list that I had given her, and he said she had been in to see him and he had been retained to represent her collaboratively. We did everything that we're supposed to do in collaboration. We hired the neutrals. We got set up. We had our initial meetings to discuss the clients and our takes on the clients, and the clients eventually got to the facilitator. We were using a licensed family counselor in that case. We knew a little bit about what their emotional states were and what their goals were in the divorce. My client again came across with, "I just want to be able to look in the mirror when we're done."

It turns out these parties had been married for twenty years, never had kids. She seemed pretty dependent on him from the facilitator's perspective, and also his. Anyway, we get to the first team meeting and she's crying. Everything we discussed, she's crying. She's just like a little well of tears falling down her face.

Finally my client leans over to me and he says, "I told you this would happen," in a really loud whisper. "I told you this would happen. Everyone's going to hate me. I'm the bad guy. She's the good guy. She's making them hate me," and I looked at the facilitator and the facilitator said, "I think it's time for a break."

I stepped outside of the room with my client. We didn't even make it down the hallway. We got far enough from the door and I closed the door so that they couldn't hear me. I said, "What's going on?" He said, "I took twenty thousand dollars out of our account." See, he had been supporting her this whole time. She was working, but he'd been putting his paycheck in the joint account the whole time, so she's paying her bills. He's paying his bills where he is, but she has access to all of their money and he had taken out the twenty thousand base, if you will, that was in there.

I said, "Well, why'd you do that?" And he said, "It was the only way I could get her to a lawyer! I'm sorry if I hurt her feelings, but I just can't take this anymore, and I needed her to go see a lawyer."

I looked at him and I said, "Wait. You said you're sorry? Can you tell her that?" He said, "Of course I can tell her that!" It was like I was being silly! Of course he could say that to her, but he hadn't. Then I said to him, "Can you put the money back?" And he said, "Of course I can put the money back." I looked at him and I said, "Okay, well let's go back in and tell them that."

So we walked in and I started to settle myself in my chair and he didn't even do that. He put his hands on the back of his chair and he leans across his chair at her, not in her face, not in her space, but just, I mean what I'm telling you right now, and he says, "I'm so sorry, Kayla. I never meant to hurt you. I just wanted you to go see a lawyer. I'll put it back." Her tears stopped. It was like someone turned off the well. Someone pulled the plug. I don't know. It was weird. Everyone in the room looked startled.

Her lawyer looked at him and actually did that taken aback kind of thing. His neck pulled his head back from the table, and he's like, "Really? Wow." The financial guy looks at him and says, "So, can you get that back in the account by five o'clock?" He's so pragmatic. "Can you get that back in the account by five pm?" And my client said, "Absolutely. I'll get it in there within an hour of leaving this room." And he did, but she didn't cry. It was weird. She didn't cry from that point on.

Now it was not an easy divorce. Don't get me wrong, but his apology went so far to make her feel better and safe and secure, which is what she needed. She just needed to feel safe, that this process was going to work for her and that at the end of the day she would be okay. In fact, that's what happened.

What was the worst courtroom divorce you've been involved in?

Joryn Jenkins: People ask me that all the time, and unfortunately there are so many contestants for that honor, not least of which is my own husband's divorce. I came in after the fact of that. He and I started dating, I think it was two months after their trial, but we spent ten years in litigation with his ex-wife until we figured out that what she really wanted was just not to pay child support! Once we figured that out, we took care of that and she never filed another motion. She had been filing a motion in court every twelve days and she never filed another one.

I think probably the one that jumps to mind is, before anyone else, I had a young woman come see me. She was the spitting image of Uma Thurman, I swear. I called my staff in to meet her right away. I said, "I know you must get this all the time!" She kind of blushed and she said, "No, not really."

She was a travel attendant and she had a fourteen-month-old. I think at the time that they started the divorce proceedings, she had left him, but the child was over two by the time I met her. She had fired her lawyer and was coming to me for a new lawyer.

We spent four years in litigation. Now remember she had already spent a year in litigation. We spent four years in litigation and it was all funded by Grandpa. Grandpa, who was the husband's father, had come to her when she delivered their son. She was just home from the hospital and he comes to visit her. There's no one else there, and he walks in the room and he says to her, "You know, you really ought to make sure you have a spare," and she looked at him. "What are you talking about?" And he says, "Well, you know, you've already had one boy, but we need another."

What he was talking about was his succession, if you will. None of his other children had children. This was the eldest son and this was the eldest son of the eldest son, and he wanted to make sure that he had an heir. I didn't get that story until we were about halfway through the four years.

We were about two years into it when she finally told me that story. She didn't think it was important, and it really wasn't, but the fact of the matter is that that gives you some idea of why Grandpa was funding this divorce proceeding.

We managed to get her majority time-sharing back then and their temporary time-sharing had been half and half, which had just killed her. She had been a stay-at-home mom for fourteen months when they started the case, so it was really hard on her.

I think she had just stopped breastfeeding. Anyway, we had gotten the case to majority time sharing. They appealed. They appealed four times and they lost every appeal.

It turns out after a while I figured out that Grandpa was actually drafting the pleadings, which everybody thinks, oh my God. That's so strange! But Grandpa was a lawyer. He was also a brigadier general, so he was not only drafting the pleadings, but he was telling the lawyers, "You will file this."

What ended up happening was, we saw pleadings that came across in really weird fonts with really weird spacing that weren't signed by the lawyers.

He would sign them as "Attorney In Fact" which I've never seen before. I understand what the legal term is, attorney in fact, and it turns out that his son had told him, "You're my attorney in fact."

We had four of Dad's lawyers quit, and at the end of the day, when I went to the court to get my legal fees from Dad instead of from my client, Mom, I put four of his attorneys on the stand to testify, and two of them testified that they quit because he was drafting the letters and the pleadings and telling them that they had to file those, and they weren't willing to do that. That case was just horrifying.

My poor client spent every penny she had. She sold her premarital condo to pay my fees. Ultimately, I think she still owed me, and this was after he contributed to her fees. I think she still owed me several hundred thousand dollars when she ended up filing bankruptcy, but we're still friends. We still talk.

One day, Dad stopped filing pleadings. We were in the middle of stuff and Dad just stopped. I talk about it. I say he went dark. I called my client after a couple of weeks and I said, "What's going on? They're not filing anything. They're not doing anything." And she said, "Oh yeah. Brandon came home the other night from his weekend at his dad's and apparently, Grandpa died."

How can readers get more information and connect with you?

For more information:
E-mail Joryn@OpenPalmLaw.com
www.NextGenerationDivorce.com
www.collaborativepractice.com

MAXINE WEISS KUNZ

A Conversation with Maxine Weiss Kunz
Weiss-Kunz & Oliver, LLC.

Maxine, tell us about your business and the types of clients that you serve?

Maxine Weiss Kunz: My business is concentrated solely in the area of family law. That includes anyone going through a divorce, and anyone who needs enforcement in post-decree measures from their divorce. I also handle parentage cases. That includes families out of wedlock. And, I handle premarital agreements (and post-nuptial agreements), adoptions, and in addition to those areas that I would term "traditional litigation," I also have a Collaborative practice and a mediation practice. Finally, I am certified as a child representative, Guardian ad Litem and/or Parenting Coordinator for the Cook County courts.

What have you found to be the biggest myths or misconceptions about your role in the process of a divorce?

Maxine Weiss Kunz: The biggest, unfortunate misconception that people have is that the lawyers might be interested in embroiling the situation, making it more contested, making it more difficult for the family. The majority of people in my legal world, especially within the network that I try to associate with, are genuinely trying to help the family. There is some hand-holding that goes along with the family law world that might not be anticipated by a litigant and sometimes that falls into the "misconception" component. I am referring to the emotional aspect of divorce, perhaps what might be confused as a therapeutic aspect. Lawyers have a lot of resources that they can provide to their clients to find help, if the client will accept the suggestion. Otherwise the client can end up angry with their lawyer for charging their normal hourly rates after they spend a half hour on the telephone venting their emotional issues. Lawyers are here to help and sometimes that means finding them other resources.

What are some of the most common fears that people have about working with someone in your profession?

Maxine Weiss Kunz: Usually people who have fears about the process are concerned about what I would call The Big Two: 1) their children; or 2) their money. If they are scared, they are often scared they are going to lose control over one of those things... either that they are going to lose control over their access to their children - or perhaps their role playing in decision making for their children – or, that they are going to lose their money. When I talk about money fears, I mean clients are often scared they will be in a financially impaired situation post-divorce, which might set them back from retirement or change their standard of living. These are the most common fears I see and work to address and resolve.

What are some of the little known pitfalls or common mistakes that you've seen divorcing couples make that you would want to make people aware of?

Maxine Weiss Kunz: This is an important question. Too often I see people mixing the children issues with the money issues; many people will be fighting for a position as it relates to their children that might not be, not only in the best interest of their children, but it might not be in the best interest of the mom or the dad who is fighting for it.

For example, I see a lot of parents who might be the higher income earners trying to posture for residential parenting time with their children, when that might not have historically been their role in the marriage. That's okay if they're genuinely able to take on that role now and put the children first. But if they're only taking that position because they want to decrease their child support obligation or maybe decrease a maintenance obligation, that's not wise for them or for their family as it's unsustainable. Children need consistency, especially in divorce.

In marriages that don't have children, couples often do not understand what "marital property" encompasses. What I mean by that is a lot of people have this perception that "My car's in my name" or "My retirement account is in my name," but if it was acquired during the marriage, a lot of times title does not matter and the asset is still marital and subject to division in the divorce. So there has to be a lot of reality testing as it relates to what is "mine" versus what is really part of the marriage or "marital property."

Can you give me an example of one of your more challenging cases that you've helped a couple with?

Maxine Weiss Kunz: The more difficult cases often involve either drug or alcohol abuse, or some kind of personality disorder, and I don't say that to point the finger. Those situations are often when people need the most help and they might be afraid to get that help. Going back to the fear question above, because of the impending divorce, these situations are really challenging because you want to find the resources for the party(s) that have the problem, and in a divorce situation they are even more likely to be resistant to help; even more resistant than they would be in an intact marriage by virtue of the fact that they're afraid of looking like the impaired party. Thus, in those cases, I like to bring in other professionals, particularly professionals involved in the Collaborative world, who understand both the therapeutic needs as well as the consequences in the divorce, and who can really balance those needs.

Since you understand both the Collaborative world and the litigation world, how do you determine which is most appropriate?

Maxine Weiss Kunz: Whenever I have an initial meeting or consultation with a client, we discuss all the various options that are available to them. We discuss traditional litigation. We discuss "What is Collaborative law?" A lot of clients have never heard of Collaborative law before meeting with me. We discuss if we should bring in a child specialist or a financial advisor, and then I look at two factors.

First, I look at what the clients are telling me they want. Do they want to have more control over the situation? Well, then they may be ideal for collaboration or mediation. Or, are they more interested in turning the reins over to the attorneys? Perhaps they have a very challenging job, and emotionally it's just easier for them to hand everything over to the attorneys; then traditional litigation is probably going to play a better role for that individual.

The key determining factor as to whether two parties can participate in the Collaborative Law Process is whether both parties are coming to the table in good faith. By good faith I mean both parties are thinking in their minds, "It is unfortunate that the marriage broke down, but now let's do what is truly best for us and our children within the confines of the law even though it might not feel good now." Versus the person thinking, "I'm so angry, I'm going to do anything I can to make your life as my divorcing spouse miserable even if that means making bad choices for my children, because it's going to hurt my ex and/or have some gain to me financially." The latter is coming to the table in bad faith. Hiding assets is obviously coming to the table in bad faith. Some kind of alternative agenda, perhaps they're already engaged to a new person, may be coming to the table in bad faith.

If we have two people who are both operating in good faith, they are strong candidates for Collaborative or Cooperative law, or attorney-assisted mediation, so long as they have an attorney on the other side who is also cognizant and genuinely aware of these resources. It's the combination of, is there good faith and who is the counsel on the other side, that determine if a case is suited for Collaborative.

Otherwise, with traditional litigation, I try to use it respectfully but that's going to be the default really. As I noted above, some couples just do not want to collaborate and that's okay, too; there are lots of tools in the toolbox if traditional litigation is needed.

You're very passionate about this. What inspired you to become a divorce professional?

Maxine Weiss Kunz: I have a background in psychology and communications. At the end of my undergraduate university career (around 2000), I sat down with the career counselor to plan for the future, and it was very obvious to both of us that I was going to continue on to some kind of additional/advanced education; the two options on the table became either clinical psychology or law. After some soul searching, I realized that I wanted to be more of an advocate than what might be termed a passive problem solver. I went the law route, and it was only natural that combined with my background that I became a family lawyer.

Can you share a lesson that you learned early on that still impacts how you perform your service today?

Maxine Weiss Kunz: It is highly important to get everything in writing. What I mean by that is if you are having a conversation with another lawyer who is representing a certain settlement position or who is representing that they will agree to proceed collaboratively or cooperatively versus traditional litigation, you need to make sure you have that in writing. Otherwise, at any time, they can pull the rug out from underneath you and deny that there was an agreement or a good faith intention. Clients do not like when their lawyer is taken by surprise.

What's one thing that we may not have covered that you could share with someone who wants a successful, stress-free divorce?

Maxine Weiss Kunz: I think the most important thing a potential litigant or party to a divorce can do is research, research, and more research before you hire your lawyer (and it doesn't have to be a Collaborative professional). Your lawyer needs to be somebody who understands the actual needs of the client, understands their goals, has the time to put in the effort to achieve those goals and communicate with the client, and somebody who has a real knowledge of the law.

One of the problems that some Collaborative attorneys encounter is when the clients reach an agreement that is difficult to enforce legally. One of the reasons I enjoy practicing both traditional and un-traditional family law (collaborative or mediation aspects being less traditional) is that it gives me a reality tester of can we put this "out-of-the-box play" into a working document, an enforceable instrument; and if we weren't doing it this way, what would a judge do? What would a traditional litigator do? Reality-testing is so important when you are outside of the sphere of the courtroom and the judge.

So how can someone find out more and connect with you?

Maxine Weiss Kunz: As far as connecting with me personally, I am easy to reach. My firm has a website. We have a 24-hour voice mail that is transcribed and emailed to us if we are not in the office. My website has a blog. I have a partner and associates in my office who can field questions if I'm not personally available. As far as knowing how to find Collaborative professionals, the generation before me is not going to like this answer, but there are so many quality resources on the internet. Even if you receive an attorney name by word of mouth/referral, which is I think the best way to seek legal counsel, you should still look them up on the internet. Go to that person's website. Look at their bio. They should have an online CV or an online profile page. What's their educational background? Have they published any articles? Are they involved in any legal committees? Have they written any appeals? Etc. Because if they have not done the dirty stuff, or have not been involved in their legal community, then you may need to question whether they are the right fit for your case.

Maxine Weiss Kunz

WEISS-KUNZ & OLIVER, LLC

110 E. Schiller Street, Ste 319

Elmhurst IL 60126

(Chicago and Park Ridge offices available by appointment)

Office: 312-605-4041

Fax: 224-241-3241

Email: mwkunz@wkofamilylaw.com

ROBERT D. BORDETTE

A Conversation with
Robert D. Bordette, CFP®, CDFA™

What do couples need to know about the divorce mediation process?

Divorce is a difficult transition for all couples, but the process does not need to be a bitter struggle. Using divorce mediation allows you to end your marriage without a lengthy court battle. Mediation puts divorcing couples in control of their fate and gives them the power to make important decisions concerning their children and property. It is growing in popularity and in many cases courts require couples to attempt mediation before moving forward with litigation.

What does the mediation process entail?

Mediation is a controlled discussion intended to create a jointly beneficial resolution for divorcing for divorcing couples. It is facilitated by a neutral third party mediator and might include individual representation for each spouse, as well as expert resources available to answer questions regarding real estate, finances or mental health. Most mediated divorces are completed over the course of several sessions that take place in a neutral location, typically the mediator's office.

Mediation begins with the decision to divorce and then the choosing of the mediator. There are many qualified mediators. Couples can be assigned a mediator by the court or can find a mediator on their own. Typically, the mediator's fees are split between the spouses.

The First Session

Mediation begins with an initial meeting of the divorcing spouses, their attorneys if they have chosen to use individual representation, and the mediator. Some mediators refer to this initial session as orientation because it allows spouses to become familiar with the mediation process. All mediations are unique, but there is structure in place to help guide the proceedings.

This initial meeting also includes advice on communication. The goal of mediation is for couples to work through their differences and reach a resolution that is mutually beneficial and ideal for their family, which requires listening, open-mindedness and flexibility. These things are explained during the initial meeting.

Additionally, the first mediation session provides an opportunity for each spouse to state his or her case. This might be done alone with the mediator, in session face-to-face with both spouses present, or in a combination of the two. The mediator usually asks clarifying questions and discusses issues that are points of agreement and contention. If any of the issues are already settled, those are put aside to be included in the final agreement.

Once a mediator has a sense of the issues in dispute, he or she discusses a plan with the divorcing spouses for resolving these issues. Additional information might be required for further discussion, so spouses are sent away with the task of gathering documents or anything else related to the issue. Often, information regarding real estate or financial matters is included in this category.

Additionally during the initial session, mediators review the paperwork and various documents associated with the filing of the divorce. If paperwork is incomplete, mediators can help couples with these materials, as long as no advice is given in favor of one spouse or the other. Mediators are legally required to remain neutral at all times.

Finding a Resolution through Communication

Robert D. Bordette: In subsequent mediation sessions, mediators work with spouses to discuss the issues in dispute and potential solutions. Spouses are encouraged to share plans for resolution and be open to compromise. These sessions are an opportunity to truly explore marital issues, such as property, joint investments, debts and loans, and custody of children (if any) and determine how these issues will be handled once the marriage has ended. Each issue might be addressed in different sessions or can be combined into as few sessions as possible. The initial meeting will have addressed a schedule and the divorcing couple is given some say in how the proceedings unfold.

Mediators prepare for subsequent meetings by reviewing the important aspects of a divorce. They analyze finances and examine the overall value of marital property. They consider where each spouse is in regard to supporting himself or herself and consider how long it would take a spouse to become self-sufficient. They take a significant look at the health and well-being of the children in the family and consider what each spouse is requesting in relation to what the children want or need.

The mediator reflects on the issues discussed during the initial meeting and how these discussions were handled. The mediator's purpose is to facilitate communication and determine if the solutions spouses consider are reasonable. To do this successfully, they must have a complete understanding of the situation and be prepared for any potential challenges.

A mediator's job is not to force couples into agreement or make decisions for them. Instead, mediators guide divorcing couples toward fair, satisfactory resolutions. Mediators can make suggestions, but they cannot offer legal advice to either spouse or tell either spouse what to do.

Once the mediation is successfully concluded, the mediator draws up a written document known as the Memorandum of Understanding (MOU) that includes the details of the divorce agreement. Each spouse has an opportunity to review the documented plan with his or her personal attorney and then an official divorce agreement is drawn up by the attorneys.

The length of mediation varies from couple to couple. Most sessions last a few hours and there can be as few as one session or as many as needed over the course of several weeks. The length of mediation depends on the complexity of the issues and the willingness of the spouses to come to agreement. In nearly every instance, though, mediation is faster than traditional litigation.

Mediation continues to grow in popularity as a means by which couples can divorce without the bitter drawn out litigation process. In the United States, nearly half of all first marriages end in divorce and nearly every one of those that are mediated are settled successfully.

Mediation is efficient and gives spouses control over the outcome of their situation. These benefits result in feelings of satisfaction and a greater likelihood the divorce agreement will not cause problems down the road.

Have you decided divorce is the only way to bring your marital strife to an end? Has your spouse presented you with a petition for divorce? Mediation can help you resolve even the most contentious matters faced by you and your soon-to-be former spouse.

To ensure your mediation is successful, you need an experienced mediator. Robert D. Bordette provides effective mediation solutions for divorcing couples. Bob helps couples talk with each other openly, directly and with compassion, guiding them to agreement on their various issues. Whether mediation is your chosen alternative to litigation or you have been ordered by the court to attempt mediation, Bob can help. At the end of the mediation process, he drafts a "memorandum of understanding" summarizing the agreement.

Why should I choose the collaborative process?

To preserve family relationships is a simple answer to the question of "Why".

According to clients who have engaged in the collaborative process, they have said the following:

- *"I would recommend the collaborative process for anyone that wants to maintain a loving environment for their children. You can get divorced, but your kids can still have a family".*

- *"Through the collaborative process we learned to work together in ways that will continue to benefit us and our children and with the help of the financial expert, we even saved money".*

- *"The collaborative process gave me the opportunity to control my own destiny".*

- *"My children were not forgotten in the divorce. This process insured they had a voice".*

- *"The partnership between the legal, financial and mental health professionals worked wonderfully for our entire family".*

Why should I choose the collaborative process instead of traditional litigation?

1. Lower Cost

The collaborative process is generally less costly and time-consuming than litigation.

2. Client Involvement

The client is a vital part of the settlement team and has a greater sense of involvement in the decision making which affects their lives.

3. Supportive Approach

Each client is supported by their lawyer and coach in a manner that still allows the attorneys to work collaboratively with one another in resolving issues.

4. Less Stress

The process is much less fear and anxiety producing than utilizing Court proceedings or the threat of such proceedings. Everyone can focus on settlement without the imminent threat of "going to Court".

5. Win-Win Climate

The Collaborative process creates a positive climate that produces a more satisfactory outcome for both parties. The possibility actually exists for participants to create a climate that facilitates "win-win" settlements.

6. Speed

The speed of the collaborative process is governed by the parties rather than court calendars.

7. Creativity

The collaborative process encourages creative solutions in resolving issues.

8. Clients in Charge

The non-adversarial nature of the collaborative process shifts decision making into the hands of the clients where it belongs, rather than into the hands of a third party (the court).

Is the Collaborative Process Right For Me?

Couples whose marriages are in trouble face many difficult decisions, all of which have the potential for serious consequences.

Some of these may be:

- Is this marriage worth saving?

- Will the children be harmed?

- What will be the ramifications of our divorce?

- How deeply will it alter our life?

You may also feel:

- Ambivalent about ending the relationship

- You are the most hurt, misunderstood, damaged, or least powerful person in the relationship

- Your partner is using the myriad of divorce counter plays as a way to stay married

- Intimidated by your partner in addressing and resolving complex and difficult issues

- We would have a great divorce if it weren't for the other party

- The divorce is your last chance to destroy the other party

How does the collaborative process work?

As in traditional family law/divorce cases, your lawyer supports only you and your spouse's lawyer supports only your spouse. In the collaborative process, both lawyers are trained to consider the other parties' perspective in order to help both of you reach agreements that accomplish the goals of both parties and preserve the welfare of the entire family.

Collaborative practitioners work as part of an inter-disciplinary network of professionals to provide expertise and advice on issues relevant to the ultimate settlement of the case.

Before the process begins, the lawyers and clients formally contract to work together to resolve the issues of the case. Both lawyers contract not to take the case to court. They sign a contract titled "Participation Agreement". In traditional litigation the divorce process begins with the filing of a lawsuit. The collaborative process begins with the signing of the Participation Agreement.

The parties also sign a document "Statement of Understanding Among Team Members". This document contains the commitment of the professionals and the parties to work together as a team with the common goal of resolution of all issues in a way that best meets the needs of all involved.

The collaborative process differs significantly from the traditional litigation process. After both parties have each retained their collaborative lawyer, the lawyers contact one another to "triage" the case. The lawyers immediately begin to address the needs of their clients by discussing their clients' needs and desires with the other lawyer.

The lawyers schedule an initial 4 way meeting which includes both lawyers and both parties. An agenda that outlines the items that will be discussed at the first meeting is sent to both parties. Any pressing issues will be covered in that first meeting, after the required participation agreements are signed.

At the first meeting, the parties will also identify the other professionals with whom they will be working. The other professionals include coaches, a child specialist if children are involved and a single financial neutral.

The collaborative process begins only with the signing of the Participation Agreement and Statement of Understanding by the attorneys and parties at their first 4 way meeting. After that first meeting, depending on the needs and desires of the parties, they may work with their coaches, the child specialist and/or the financial neutral before seeing their attorneys again.

In this way, costs are minimized as the professional with the appropriate expertise deals with their particular area. For example, the coaches will help the parties address their communication issues in order to assist them in creating a parenting plan for their children. The child specialist will hear from the children and offer feedback to the coaches and parties to insure that the children's developmental needs are considered.

The financial neutral will gather information from the parties and work with them and the attorneys to craft a financial plan based on a realistic financial picture.

The meetings in the collaborative process promote improved communication and cooperation. The collaborative environment is one that fosters informed analysis and reasoning. In the process, the professionals and parties generate options and create a positive context for settlement. The parties always retain control over their outcome. The commitment to continued cooperation, even if communication becomes difficult, increases the likelihood of a solution that builds a foundation for the future of the family even as the parents begin separate lives.

Ultimately, once all issues are resolved, the attorneys draft a settlement agreement and the pleadings necessary to obtain a divorce. The pleadings are filed jointly and indicate to the court that the parties have reached an agreement through the collaborative process. If possible, the attorneys file a Motion for Judgment on the Pleadings, a document which allows a Final Judgment and Decree of Divorce to be granted by the court without the necessity of a court appearance.

If the court will not grant a final divorce in that manner, one or both of the parties will appear in court for the short amount of time it takes for the court to accept their settlement agreement and grant them a final divorce.

Who practices collaborative family law?

All professionals who practice collaborative family law focus on the family in different ways. The lawyers have an expertise in domestic relations (family law), the mental health professionals are well-versed in family systems, and the financial neutral has working knowledge of asset divisions, child support guidelines, cash flow analyses, and basic tax implications of support payments.

They are specially trained in the collaborative process, commit to the Standards of Conduct and follow the Guidelines of Practice established by the Collaborative Law Institute of Georgia.

The professionals practicing collaboratively commit to the process as well as its outcome. Their training and education encourages mature, co-operative and non-combative behavior. They contract not to participate should the case go to court and in that way have a stake in the success of the process.

The professionals who practice collaboratively protect the privacy and dignity of all involved in the process. They uphold high standards of integrity and, if inconsistencies and miscalculations occur, seek to correct them.

Collaborative practitioners expend as much effort working toward settlement of your case as they would to prepare for and conduct a trial. Together with their clients, the collaborative professional expends his or her time and energy on settlement, parenting plans, financial analysis, and education.

The parties provide complete, honest and open disclosure of all relevant information without formal proceedings. The inter-disciplinary network of divorce professionals and their clients are committed to finding creative ways to achieve and implement a settlement that will be best for the family.

To learn more, visit: http://www.u2agree.com

SCOTT TUCKER

A Conversation with Scott Tucker
Scott Tucker Solutions

Tell us about your business and the types of clients that you serve?

Scott Tucker: I'm a financial and retirement planner in Chicago. I help people 55-years and older. I specialize in helping couples and even divorcing couples. What sometimes happens when their kids are leaving the nest and folks are fed up with one another, sadly, they sometimes choose to file for a divorce.

What do you feel are the biggest myths or misconceptions about the role of a fiduciary as it plays in a divorce situation?

Scott Tucker: What I recommend when folks are considering divorce if they've gotten that far, of course, I like the idea of having one attorney manage the divorce and come down in the middle. I think it's a great way to save money, especially when funds may be limited or when you're trying to plan for retirement, college costs or whatever the case may be. I think the same thing comes into play when you're dealing with a financial advisor that's helping you work through your divorce.

I'm a fiduciary advisor, meaning that I'm legally bound to do the best thing for the client. I like working with folks that are amiable in their divorce and can say, "Let's just do what's fair. Let's draw it down the middle." Then, I can develop a plan that protects both parties and gives them the best outcome possible and especially if there are kids involved, that's another consideration.

Are there any controversial topics that you've heard of regarding this or any common misinformation that you've seen out there that you'd like to address?

Scott Tucker: I think the closest things to the question you ask would be the idea that we have to lawyer-up and we have to duke it out and we have to each have our own lawyer. We have to each have our own CPA, or each of us have to have our own financial advisor. All you're doing is just doubling your costs. You're getting divorced, you're already going to be doubling your housing costs in many respects because you're going to have two households now with no additional income.

The tooth fairy didn't come and drop off $1,000,000 in your lap. To add unnecessary costs for the attorney's fees for a divorce, for a CPA or a financial advisor, to just double all these costs, doesn't make any sense to me. That would be the answer to that.

What would you say are some of the most common fears people have about their finances when it comes to divorce?

Scott Tucker: One of the greatest fears would be, "Does Bob have a secret account he hasn't told me about?" Or, "Does Mary have a secret account she hasn't told me about?" Usually one person is more involved in the finances or is more financially savvy. It can be, "Is that person going to take advantage of me?" What I like about being a fiduciary and helping couples that are divorcing, is I'm there in a capacity that each person can trust that they're going to get the solution that's best for each of them and it's going to be fair.

What are some little known pitfalls or common mistakes that you've seen made when people are going through a divorce as it pertains to their finances?

Scott Tucker: Beneficiary designations. There are so many. Let's say we divvy up the accounts. You get your IRA. You get your pension. We divvy these things up amongst these two folks in a way that's equitable. We also have to remember to look at beneficiary designations. You wouldn't want, after you've already divided everything, you wouldn't want your IRA, if you pass away, going to your ex-wife versus your new wife, or to your ex-husband versus your new husband. The beneficiary designations are a thing that people overlook quite a bit.

Could you give us an example of a way that you can help a divorcing couple go through their financial situation, perhaps a case study or an example?

Scott Tucker: We actually take a financial inventory and get down on paper what are all the assets, how do each of them function. Some things are very complicated like Social Security. There are all sorts of rules of. You can take a spousal benefit if you were married 10 years and so on.

There are all these little wrinkles and loopholes and catches to all this stuff. That kind of thing can come into play for Social Security and similar issues can arise when it comes to pensions, where there are spousal benefits available.

We really need to go through everything with a fine tooth comb and make sure that we consider all the angles and all the issues involved. It's really quite a complex situation.

Scott, how did you personally get started in your profession? What inspired you?

Scott Tucker: I always wanted to help people with their finances. Finance has really been something that's been interesting to me. I've always been interested in helping families with their finances. Some folks want to go work in corporate America. I don't find that to be very exciting. It can be financially rewarding to do that, but I think you're going in, punching the clock every day, and working for somebody else. Feeling that you might make a difference for a corporation or for a shareholder, but you don't really know those people.

Part of what I like about my practice is I know everybody that I help face-to-face. I have a real relationship with all my clients. It's a lot more interesting to work with individuals and families than it is to work for a corporation in my mind.

Can you share a lesson that you learned early on that still impacts how you perform your service today?

Scott Tucker: I guess I would say, "Don't assume anything." That can come in any area. There are the common things, like the millionaire next door that I love. Don't assume that folks that appear to be simply dressed or live simply don't have any money. It's usually those are the folks who do have the money. Don't assume that a gentleman with a Rolex has $1,000,000. He may have $5.00. That's something right there.

Also, when it comes to stock market risks. Some folks may have a great risk tolerance. You might sit down with them, and they may say, "I lost $200,000 in the stock market in 2008." To me, that sounds horrible, but to them, it may just be a statement. "I lost $200,000." They're okay with it because they came back or whatnot.

I'll ask folks. This is one example, but I'll ask folks, "Oh, $200,000, is that a little or a lot to you?" It may not be a big deal. It may be that they were suicidal or maybe they said, "Oh well, it's going to come back and I have ten more years to work." I don't assume anything.

I met with a client recently who is looking at about a $5,000,000 estate tax. This couple, their daughter will have to pay when she inherits the properties, the real estate. I said, "You know, you guys are worth about $20,000,000. Even if she has to pay $5,000,000 or $7,000,000 because these rates may be changing in the future, she's still going to have $13,000,000, $15,000,000. She'll still be okay. Is that okay with you to just leave it as is?"

Both parties objected right away. "No, we don't want to leave it as is. We can't stand giving the government any more money." Then, we developed an estate tax plan. A lot of folks may come to me to help with their divorce but they may leave with solutions to problems they didn't even know they had.

Is there one thing that we may not have covered that you could share with somebody's who wanting a successful, stress-free divorce as it relates to your field in finance?

Scott Tucker: I think I would say, "Don't leave it up to your attorney." No matter how good that attorney is, don't leave it up to an attorney to cover these areas. The attorney or any professional could be distracted by focusing on what they do best. Same thing could be for your CPA. Your CPA, some CPAs are terrific at doing taxes after the year has ended.

Some CPAs are great at doing tax planning before the year starts. Some CPAs are really savvy when it comes to these financial issues and will work hand-in-hand with your advisor. Some CPAs won't do that at all.

You may leave things undone that should be addressed before the divorce is finalized. Once you've got that Divorce

Decree, your divorce is final, try making changes to it. Very, very difficult, if not impossible.

How can our readers find out more and connect with you, Scott Tucker?

Scott Tucker: Readers can go to my website at www.ScottTuckerSolutions.com or they can contact me at 773-230-2682.

THERESA BERAN KULAT

A Conversation with
Theresa Beran Kulat, J.D
Trinity Family Law

Ending your primary relationship creates all sorts of challenges. When you take a holistic approach and stay grounded in your values, you improve the likelihood of getting through it with grace and ease.

Theresa Beran Kulat, J.D. used her divorce as a vehicle for personal growth. She provides her clients with an environment, resources, and the legal representation they need to create healthy new lives.

Tell us about Trinity Family Law and how you approach your work.

Theresa Beran Kulat: I started the law firm in 2003 shortly after my own divorce when the Collaborative movement was in its infancy. From the beginning, I focused solely on the Collaborative Process and other non-adversarial divorce approaches. For me personally, non-adversarial law fits with who I am.

My mind is focused and, with law school and years of experience, I know how to analyze very complex problems. I also have highly developed "soft skills" from my background as a retreat leader and life coach. The Collaborative Process allows me to use both the left and the right sides of my brain, combining both of these skill sets.

How does this look in practice?

Theresa Beran Kulat: It begins with our location and office environment. We prefer the "home converted to office space" to an office building. In fact, when people walk in the door, many often comment that they relax. They expect a sterile, corporate environment. Instead, they enter a place that reminds them of someone's home. Everyone in the practice knows it is their job to put people at ease.

When I meet a prospective client for the first time, I listen to their story in order to understand their unique concerns. Then I explain the way divorce happens legally in the State of Illinois, not "what they are going to get," but "how they could possibly get there."

Uncertainty about the law is only one aspect of the anxiety people feel at that initial meeting. They often struggle with much more personal issues that concern identity... ("We've been a couple so long, I don't know who I am."), family ("How do I tell the children?") and religious beliefs ("I am afraid to tell my parents."). Underlying these issues are feelings of guilt, anger, and a myriad of other emotions.

In our practice, we acknowledge these concerns and emotions. I tell my client that, as their attorney, I will walk alongside them through their divorce. My hope for each of my clients is that when the divorce is complete, they feel stronger and more confident about the future than on the first day we met.

Tell us how you got into this line of work.

Theresa Beran Kulat: As a young child, I experienced the fall out of divorce gone bad.

My father's parents divorced in the 1940's when he and his sister were very young (4 and 6 years old) because there had been infidelity. The judge, rather than giving either parent custody, sent them to an orphanage in the area. While each parent could visit the children, they never saw themselves as a "family".

Sadly, my grandparents never let go of their anger. When I was old enough to notice, they had been divorced for over twenty years and still would not speak to each other. Over the years, it was awkward for everyone as we accommodated their wishes when planning any family gathering. They were never in the same place at the same time. At Christmas, Grandpa would come to our house and Grandma would go to my aunt's house. If there was a party that both attended, like a graduation party, they would not be in the same room or the same floor.

If Grandma walked into the kitchen, Grandpa would leave and go to the family room. If she went there, he'd walk outside. Needless to say, it was uncomfortable for everyone; you could feel the tension in the air.

When I learned about the Collaborative Process, I could see that it offers people the opportunity to heal these deep wounds. I know the traditional legal system is designed to find fault – but in families, finding "fault" actually makes things worse.

Years later, when my husband and I divorced, I knew our future had to be different for our sake and the sake of our two boys. We needed a process that allowed for us to maintain a relationship so we could co-parent our children so that we could be in the same room at graduations and other life events without the tension that was so prevalent at family holidays when I was growing up. I heard about the

Collaborative Process and knew that this was the model for us to use.

After my divorce, I took the first training offered in Illinois and established a law practice focused on non-adversarial divorce. In the ensuing years, I have helped many clients – and indirectly others in their family and circle of friends.

I also am committed to helping spread the word about Collaborative so that it is the first option people consider when divorcing. I do this through my law practice, as well as through my involvement with the Collaborative Law Institute of Illinois, the professional association for attorneys, mental health professionals and financial specialists here in Illinois. I've held many leadership positions in the organization, including serving as president.

What is the key to a no-stress or low-stress divorce?

Theresa Beran Kulat: Divorce is, without a doubt, stressful and each party will experience stress differently. When people come in, the stress comes from many directions, including uncertainty about the future and not understanding the legal process.

The key is to build self-awareness. Know thyself.

- What is important to you? Your children's well-being? Your ability to retire at 65? Your health? Your freedom? The ability to follow your dreams?

- Being conscious of your values and choosing a divorce process that aligns with those values and that gives you tools to manage the stress of divorce. Ending a marriage means that many important aspects of life will be taken apart and put back together in a new way – finances, living arrangements, relationships with children and family of origin, time and – most importantly – identity. If a person can get in touch with who they are and who they want to be when it's over, their prospect for a "good" divorce increases.

My specific advice to someone getting a divorce: Recognize that you have a choice in how you respond to the stress. Look at each component that is contributing to it so that you can address each part rather than trying to tackle everything at once. This will go a long way in reducing stress levels. In our practice, we work with clients to do that – we help them understand the legal process, give them a voice (e.g., walk them through options at each decision point so that they can make an informed decision), and suggest tools and habits that will help (for example, get back to the gym).

You are a Collaborative Lawyer – is that a "no stress" or "low stress" process?

Theresa Beran Kulat: Some stress in divorce comes from being out of control. Here I like to quote the Serenity Prayer: "Grant me Serenity to accept the things I cannot change, Courage to change the things I can, and Wisdom to know the difference."

In divorce, there are things you cannot change – the past, your bank account balances, the words in the statute book. Trying to change them or complaining because you can't change them will cause stress. Taking on those things you can change – how you communicate with your spouse, whether or not you work outside the home, and whether or not you will stay in the marital home – that will empower you.

But how do you know which is which? Wisdom. In this department, you may need assistance. A lawyer whose values align with yours can help you decide if keeping the marital home is wise – what are the various consequences of that decision? A financial advisor can give you advice on how to structure your post-divorce portfolio in order to retire. A good therapist/divorce coach can teach you new ways of relating to your soon-to-be-ex-spouse.

Change usually brings up discomfort. With the right support, you will increase your ability to make good choices and eventually reduce stress. This can have lasting benefits in that the coping tools, communication skills, and other techniques learned during your divorce can be carried forward into other situations and relationships.

Before we explore the Collaborative Process further, can you give folks an overview of how the legal divorce process works?

Theresa Beran Kulat: First a few general concepts... Divorce law is state specific. So the rules in one state may differ from those in another. Also, most divorces never go to trial. So while the laws of your particular state may shed light on how the "powers that be" think things should work out, most cases – over 95% – are settled out of court. While you may be completely emotionally divorced from your spouse and might have taken steps to separate your finances, in order to be legally divorced, papers must be filed with your local court system and formalized by a judge in order for the divorce to be legally recognized. That is the end of the process a judge pronounces a couple "divorced."

What is the process that a couple uses to get to that point?

Theresa Beran Kulat: Truth be told, there are a variety of ways to get there. If the decision to divorce is mutual and there is a high degree of trust and relatively little complexity, two people could probably sit at their kitchen table and work out how to divide their assets and liabilities. If they both work, and/or they share similar values on how to raise children, many issues could be resolved on their own. They could then call up a trusted local attorney to write down their agreements and help them enter the papers.

What if they don't trust each other? What if one person has been in control of all the money, or domestic violence is happening?

Theresa Beran Kulat: The court system exists to protect people when necessary. So, yes, if a person is facing divorce and they fear for their safety or believe that their spouse has squandered family resources, they should retain an aggressive divorce attorney.

That lawyer will do their best to hold the other spouse accountable, using formal discovery – things like subpoenas, depositions, interrogatories – which means the financial disclosure process will be supervised by the court system to increase reliability. If someone has been subjected to domestic violence they want an attorney who can obtain an order of protection to help keep them safe.

How does the Collaborative Process apply as a divorce option?

Theresa Beran Kulat: The Collaborative Process actually helps couples whose level of conflict falls between these two extremes. Most folks want to work things out with their spouse but need guidance. They don't want to go to battle, but they don't want to be taken advantage of either.

Can you please describe how Collaborative Divorce works?

Theresa Beran Kulat: In a Collaborative Divorce Process both spouses have attorneys. All four people commit to settling the case outside of court. Typically, clients meet one-on-one with their respective attorney to discuss details of the case, any decisions they need to make, and even communication strategies.

Going back to the image of walking with people through the divorce process, we want to help our clients understand their options and potential outcomes of their actions. This is key, because in addition to one-on-one meetings, both attorneys and their clients meet in a series of settlement conference meetings to work through the issues and reach decisions. Financial disclosures are thorough yet voluntary. We take a problem-solving approach and utilize additional neutral professionals (e.g., financial neutrals, child specialists), if necessary.

One key feature is that the Collaborative Process guidelines are spelled out in writing and everyone agrees that, if the case does not settle, the Collaborative lawyers are disqualified from representing either of these two people in a litigated divorce. These guidelines are summarized in a Participation Agreement which all parties sign at the first meeting.

When you say "problem-solving approach," what do you mean?

Theresa Beran Kulat: Let's use the example of the marital home – this one "thing" connects to so many aspects of the family. The children may go to public school based on the location of the home. Often it represents a significant financial asset of the family. Sometimes it is a significant liability. In all cases, two adults used to live in and contribute to the running of the house. After divorce, there will be two homes.

In Collaborative Divorce, we take a lot of time learning what both people want and need in terms of housing – the financial and emotional aspects, how it relates to their employment and to the children, in order to determine what to do with the house.

In a highly contentious, litigated divorce, the judge says "Sell it and split the proceeds." Their lawyers can try to convince the judge to give their client what they want regardless of the impact on the other spouse or the children.

In the Collaborative Process, we always want both parents to maintain strong relationships with the children and we want a financially viable solution for both parents. So we talk about lots of different options with respect to the house.

Sometimes a couple decides that one spouse will buy the other out of the house. Sometimes they hold it jointly for a number of years. Sometimes they decide to sell. But the key is that THEY decide to sell. They are not forced to sell by an outsider.

Our process is driven by the parties' goals and values, not what people think the judge might do. In fact, at the beginning, we outline what our client's most important goals and needs are; these goals and needs then become, in a sense, a vision that we are striving for during settlement discussions.

Are there are other options, similar to the Collaborative Process, that help keep decision-making in the divorcing couple's hands?

Theresa Beran Kulat: Other non-adversarial divorce processes include mediation and uncontested divorce.

In mediation, couples, with or without their own attorneys, hire a neutral mediator to reach agreement on various aspects of their divorce. The mediator facilitates their conversation and makes sure that they cover all the topics that need to be resolved.

A Memorandum of Understanding prepared by the mediator details the specific agreements. From there, the couple can, depending on the rules of their jurisdiction, either enter the documents themselves or hire a single attorney to complete the process. An attorney who acts as the couple's mediator cannot represent either party as their divorce attorney.

In an uncontested divorce, one spouse retains an attorney and the other spouse represents himself/herself. This approach typically works when the parties have reached agreement on their own or with a mediator on all the key issues, including how assets will be divided and where any minor children will reside. The single attorney facilitates their communication, drafts the legal documents, and takes them through the court system.

Is there anything else you would like others know about the Collaborative Process or divorce in general?

Theresa Beran Kulat: When I established Trinity Family Law over 10 years ago, we created a mission statement that continues to guide our firm: "Empower people in the divorce process and other legal matters to negotiate agreements that enable them to build healthy new lives, prosper financially, and co-parent children effectively."

These words truly embody what I believe about divorce: it is a transformative process. It will be a challenge like no other most people have encountered. Choosing the right process and the attorney that most reflects your values and goals - and acknowledges your situation - is key to people feeling supported during this transformation. Bottom line, people who are divorcing should do their homework and learn their options.

How can someone find out more and connect with you?

Theresa Beran Kulat: Trinity Family Law is located in the western suburbs of Chicago, in Downers Grove, Illinois, and we work with clients throughout the Chicago area. Our clients include professionals, many of whom own their own businesses. We do great work with parents of young children, as well as empty nesters.

Our website, www.TrinityFamilyLaw.com, is a good place to learn more about our firm and non-adversarial divorce. We can also be reached at 630-960-4656.

JENNIFER FAILLA

A Conversation with Jennifer Failla
Strada Wealth Management

Jennifer, tell us about Strada Wealth Management and the types of clients you serve.

Jennifer Failla: We are a fee-only, registered investment advisory service company that only serves families in some sort of marital transition. Specifically prenuptial agreements, divorce and martial mediation, so for those families that want to stay married but have a financial impasse or something they're trying to work through and they need somebody with strong financial acumen to guide them through that decision-making process.

In the divorce practice, we specifically help people develop viable settlement options, so we call it settlement option generations through our PlanningThruDivorce process, which is a trademarked process that we use.

What have you found to be the biggest or most common challenge that you hear your clients face?

Jennifer Failla: I think the biggest challenge over the years that I've been doing this, and I've been doing this full-time since 2006, is the misunderstood sense of entitlement. People come in, whether it's for premarital or marital mediation, and specifically around divorce, there's a misunderstood sense of entitlement around what is owed to me or what is mine or what should be mine based on misconceptions around the law, and/or what their friends have garnered from their negotiations.

Can you address that a little and give us some examples, perhaps?

Jennifer Failla: Yes. A lot of people, when they're entering, first of all, I think everybody understands that divorce is one of the more stressful things a person can go through in their lives. We at our office tell people that it's the largest financial transaction of your life because not just one aspect of your financial life is in flux, but all of them are in flux. Everything is moving. It's all moving puzzle board.

When you go to buy a house, you're just buying a house and so you're kind of going to work every day and you're stressed about the idea of buying a house, but that's only one financial aspect of your life. When you're going through divorce, your credit, your income, your savings, your living situation, what you've done to save for retirement, it's all suddenly in flux and all suddenly changing.

A lot of people come into the office and they feel that based on what they've heard or what they've read or how long they've been married, that they are entitled to certain assets and/or rights and/or income and support. Our biggest challenge initially is educating people around the fact that it's not about entitlement, it's about what's sustainable. That is a hard emotional barrier to overcome at times for clients.

For example, you might be entitled to spousal support, let's say, but the finances of the family just can't support it. We in our office have a conversation around letting the numbers tell the story, and we forget that with a divorce there is still the same marital income coming in and now there's multiple sets of expenses. There's a real education hurtle to overcome initially around that entitlement misconception.

That's really sage advice. What are some of the most common fears that you've found your clients have coming in and meeting with you?

Jennifer Failla: That's a great question. Actually that's a great question because in the early days when I first started this work and I thought I knew it all, I was young, I didn't have gray hair. I thought everybody's fear is going to be how they are going to live to retirement. As a money manager we tend to think how am I going to sustain a life after the divorce in terms of even income? That is actually not the number one fear that I've seen since 2008.

What I am finding is people are very fearful of how they're going to continue healthcare. I hear it over and over again. It's the number one aspect of their financial lives that we have to address immediately.

It's how we're going to address healthcare for themselves and, or their children after the divorce, because what you think is a viable option, maybe using COBRA because COBRA is a program that somebody who divorces can stay on for about three years and your premiums can be a max of 102% of what you were paying before to cover administration expenses.

However, we sometimes forget after three years, you're three years older, it's hard to go get healthcare if you're not on a group program, and pricing individual care three years later is a lot riskier than pricing it today.

So yes, the healthcare situation tends to be the number one aspect of their financial existence that we are seeing over and over again keeping people up at night.

Over the years I'm sure you've seen mistakes people have made and pitfalls. Are there any common mistakes that you see that you could help people avoid?

Jennifer Failla: It's interesting because I've made mistakes obviously over the years. One of my professional mistakes I think is you can't assume that what you think is important for one family is going to be important for them. As a professional, and I could see lawyers getting caught into this and other financial professionals getting caught into this, back to what I was saying earlier, what I might think would stress a family out does not necessarily stress a family out.

I honestly think back to that entitlement conversation, the number one thing if I could stress to people going into any marital transition, whether it be a prenuptial agreement, a mediation around a big decision, inheritance, a financial windfall, and, or divorce, specifically if you got to forget about what your preconceived notions are because just like in raising kids or in running your own home, what works for you might not work for somebody else.

What your family can sustain might not be sustainable for somebody else. There have been so many times people have walked into my office and said, "I have to stay," for example, "in the marital home." This seems to be an overused example Mark, but "I have to stay in the marital home," whichever spouse. "My kids go to school in this district." That might not be financially feasible.

I think the best advice I can give people over and over again when they're entering this process, is throw away what you think is normal. Just throw it out of your head and try to keep a really open mind around any slate of ideas and exploring those ideas so that they could be viable options and still be sustainable for your family.

Back to that house example. If a family comes in and says, "We need to keep our kids in this school district, and I want them to stay in this home because they're comfortable in this home." Well it could be a smaller home in the same district but not in the same house, that's financially more feasible for both parties.

What I explain to families is, if you are stressed out about finances, and you are stressed out about how to get your health insurance, and you're stressed out about how to make your bills, you are not going to be worried about your investments, your retirement and your portfolio.

Take that one step further, if you're stressed out about your finances, how to get your health insurance and how to make your bills, you're not going to be a very effective parent. This is an investment, this time, taking all those preconceived notions out and thinking what we could do. Yes it's an unfortunate situation, and yes there's a marital division happening. What can we do to set up both sides for ultimate, sustainable, financial success? Sustainable is the big word, right?

I'd imagine that the thought of the entire divorce process can be overwhelming for folks. Can you tell us how your method gives your clients calm and clarity?

Jennifer Failla: Yes. We agree with you in the aspect of it is daunting. It is a daunting thought when somebody tells you every aspect of your financial life is now in flux. We have found over the years that paralyzes people into complete inaction because it's too much to bear, to pull your credits and research your insurance and do all that. We have trademarked a process called PlanningThruDivorce, and our motto in our office is we basically tell people, "How do you eat an elephant? It's one bite at a time." We break down the different aspects of your life into subsections, if you will. It sounds trite but it works. How do we tackle the health insurance day one? Well, we start researching your options. We start getting an education around what you have and what you need. We start looking at open market versus close market versus COBRA so that you're educated and informed as to what your options are and to what to talk about when you're starting to do a settlement option generation.

Then we move on to the next topic, which is cash management. We look at income, expenses. What is it that you truly need to sustain and survive? We do a lot of work with clients in this area on vision.

We have clients do vision boards. I don't know if you've ever heard of that, where you literally start to map out what you want for yourself in the next year. Is it school, is it a new job, where do you envision living, how do you envision your new life to look, now that a spouse is not going to be in it? Are you going to pick up a new hobby?

These are the things we look at in the cash management area of analysis so that people can start really visualizing what they want, and finding fun in what I think could be a very boring process of looking at income and expenses. How does it involve the kids, whatnot.

Then we start tackling the assets and the liabilities, specifically around credits. We really break things down into manageable sections and give people achievable goals within those subsections, and we're very homework-oriented.

If I find my spouse sitting in my conference room table or both are weak in a certain area, we assign them homework around researching that subject and guide them in getting educated so they feel better about it.

A lot of times people are paralyzed into inaction because they have fear, and fear comes from not understanding or not getting the education so we're very education driven, process driven, and breaking it down into small, manageable parts.

Great. How did you get started in this field? What inspired you to get into this line of work?

Jennifer Failla: There's two areas that I could really tap into on that. I was the product of a 1980s divorce, late '70s, early '80s divorce, and anybody that is born in 1965 onward understands how costly and contentious those were at the time. Ours was no better. My mother and father made it into the law books in the state that we resided in, that's how bad it was. I remember my mother having zero financial acumen.

At age six I was helping her pay bills, reminding her to pay bills. I remember lights getting turned off, us not having food to put food in the refrigerator, and the reality of the situation was Mark, my mother got everything. My father only got his business at the end of the day, but she had no education around how to manage it and how to sustain it for herself.

Then back in 2006 and '07, I was managing money for clients, working with a big lawyer house, and I started to see decrees come in after the divorce was settled, and there were a lot of egregious errors in the decrees in the sense that clients who were under 59 1/2 couldn't access their funds.

They were living in houses they couldn't sustain because the alimony couldn't support it but they were insistent on getting the marital home, and so I started calling attorneys at that point and saying, "You know, we should really try to help them while they're negotiating their settlement, pulling in while they're negotiating their settlement and see if it's sustainable from a comprehensive financial planning perspective."

Then I opened up my own firm in 2008 and decided to dedicate only to those families that were going through that kind of transition.

Is there one thing that we may not have covered that you could share with someone who wants to have a successful and stress-free divorce?

Jennifer Failla: We touched on it, but I think it is time for a divorce revolution. It has to come from our families. It's not going to come from the legal community and I don't think it's going to come from the financial community. Our families that are divorcing have to demand that their professionals work for their best interests.

The families that are going through this transition have to demand, and understand that this is not a process they can hand to somebody else. This is not a process you walk into somebody's office and hand it to me and say, "Figure it out."

When you get married you're intimately involved in the marriage process. You see that, because you write around receptions, and weddings and whatnot. You know how involved people get in the process of getting married. In this transition, people need to be as intimately involved in this transition as they are when they're getting married.

It is unrealistic, it is naïve, and it's not smart to walk into somebody's office and hand it to another professional and expect them to get for you what you quote, unquote deserve, and are entitled to because you've handed the process over to somebody else and this is a process you need to control.

The reader, our clients, the consumer, the person who's paying our bills needs to control, but still be involved in because you can't expect any one professional to know what you need after your 35 years of marriage in two hour consults and 10-hour engagements and 20-hour engagements. This is still something that requires your time, energy and attention. With it being the largest financial transaction of your life, which I've just mentioned, it merits the attention.

I think that is one of the biggest ways we could be disruptive in this industry, is by arming our families with the data, tools and information they need to remain involved and in control of their processes to make the best decisions for themselves that are sustainable and in their best interest.

Jennifer, how can someone find out more and connect with you?

Jennifer Failla: We have a website.

www.stradamanagement.com tells you all about our services and what we can do to help families. We help families write prenuptial agreements. I know they're not fun, but we try put a lot of fun back in them.

We help families in marital mediation who want to stay married but are trying to get through a financial impasse, and of course we focus on our work on families going through a divorce.

You can learn all about us on our website and then I have a toll-free number and you can follow me on Twitter at @planthrudivorce.

ABOUT THE AUTHOR

Mark Imperial is a Best Selling Author, Syndicated Business Columnist, Syndicated Radio Host, and internationally recognized Stage, Screen, and Radio Host of numerous business shows spotlighting leading experts, entrepreneurs, and business celebrities.

His passion is discovering noteworthy business owners, professionals, experts, and leaders who do great work, and sharing their stories and secrets to their success with the world on his syndicated radio program titled "Remarkable Radio".

Mark is also the media marketing strategist and voice for some of the world's most famous brands. You can hear his voice over the airwaves weekly on Chicago radio and worldwide on iHeart Radio.

Mark is a Karate black belt, teaches kickboxing, loves Thai food, House Music, and his favorite TV show is infomercials.

Learn more:

www.MarkImperial.com
www.ImperialAction.com
www.RemarkableRadioShow.com

www.ingramcontent.com/pod-product-compliance
Lightning Source LLC
Chambersburg PA
CBHW071916200326
41519CB00016B/4628

* 9 7 8 0 9 9 9 8 7 0 8 5 1 5 *